Celebrating Sikh FESTIVALS

NICK HUNTER

raintree

a Capstone company — publishers for children

Raintree is an imprint of Capstone Global Library Limited, a company incorporated in England and Wales having its registered office at 7 Pilgrim Street, London, EC4V 6LB – Registered company number: 6695582

www.raintree.co.uk
myorders@raintree.co.uk

Text © Capstone Global Library Limited 2016
The moral rights of the proprietor have been asserted.

Edited by James Benefield
Designed by Steve Mead
Original illustrations © Capstone Global Library Limited
Picture research by Eric Gohl
Production by Helen McCreath
Originated by Capstone Global Library Limited
Printed and bound in Dubai

ISBN 978 1 406 29769 0 (hardback)
19 18 17 16 15
10 9 8 7 6 5 4 3 2 1

ISBN 978 1 406 29776 8 (paperback)
20 19 18 17 16
10 9 8 7 6 5 4 3 2 1

British Library Cataloguing in Publication Data
A full catalogue record for this book is available from the British Library.

Acknowledgements
Alamy: Ajith Saju, 22, Art Directors & TRIP, 6, 24, Eye Ubiquitous, 11, Galopin, 30, India/Gapper, 19; Capstone Studio: Karon Dubke, 16–17 (all), 28–29 (all), 40–41 (all); Dreamstime: Dariusz Renke, 5, Dmitrii Fadeev, 4, Mohamad Ridzuan Abdul Rashid, 39, Picstudio, 10; Getty Images: Photofusion, 38, Stringer/Narinder Nanu, cover, The Washington Post/Marvin Joseph, 37; Glow Images: Robert Harding/Annie Owen, 26; iStockphoto: Kulpreet Photography, 27; Newscom: EPA/Raminder Pal Singh, 25, EPA/Shabbir Hussain Imam, 21, Photoshot/Andy Barnes B200, 13, Picture Alliance/Godong/Philippe Lissac, 14, 23, 35, Reuters/Pakistan/Stringer, 18, Sipa USA/Pacific Press, 9, ZUMA Press/Brian Cahn, 15, ZUMA Press/Kabaddi, 33, ZUMA Press/Manny Crisostomo, 42, ZUMA Press/Paul Kitagaki Jr., 12, ZUMA Press/Stephen Simpson, 20; Shutterstock: Hong Vo, 44, m.bonotto, 31; SuperStock: age fotostock/Philippe Michel, 32, age fotostock/Yoko Aziz, 7.

Design Elements: Shutterstock

We would like to thank Peggy Morgan for her invaluable help in the preparation of this book.

SAFETY TIPS FOR THE RECIPES
Trying new recipes is fun, but before you start working in the kitchen, keep these safety tips in mind:
- Always ask an adult for permission, especially when using the hob, oven or sharp knives.
- At the hob, always point saucepan handles away from the edge. Don't keep flammable materials, such as towels, too close to the burners. Have a fire extinguisher nearby. Don't lean too close when you lift a lid off a pan – steam can cause burns, too. Always use oven gloves when taking dishes out of the oven.
- Wash your hands before you work, and wash your workspace and utensils after you are done. Cook foods completely. Don't use expired or spoiled food. Be careful when you cut with knives.
- Work with an adult – together you can both learn about religions of the world through food!

CONTENTS

Some words are shown in bold, **like this**. You can find out what they mean by looking in the glossary.

INTRODUCING SIKHISM

The Sikh religion was founded just over 500 years ago by **Guru** Nanak (1469–1539). This makes it much more recent than the other world religions: Buddhism, Christianity, Hinduism, Islam and Judaism. Sikhs call their religion Gurmat, which means "the way of the Guru". A Guru is a **spiritual** teacher. The name Sikh comes from the Punjabi word for a learner.

⌃ These young Sikhs attend a procession in Coventry in England.

What do Sikhs believe?

Sikhs believe in one god called Waheguru, which means "Wonderful Lord" or "Wonderful Teacher". Sikhs also follow the teachings of 10 human Gurus. These men led the religion in its early years and played important roles in defining its teachings. Sikhs worship at a **gurdwara**. This translates as a door or house to the Guru, and is where Sikhs keep their holy book.

The Guru Granth Sahib

The **Guru Granth Sahib** is the holy book of the Sikh religion. Sikhs believe that this book contains the words of their Gurus and other holy people. Sikhs read the Guru Granth Sahib regularly at home and at the gurdwara. Guru Arjan, the fifth human Guru, first collected the writings in the Guru Granth Sahib in the early 1600s. Guru Gobind Singh later revised them.

The spread of Sikhism

The Sikh religion spread from the **Punjab** region in what is now northern India and Pakistan. Today, there are around 22 million Sikhs living in India. Sikh communities can be found in many countries around the world. For example, more than 420,000 Sikhs live in the UK.

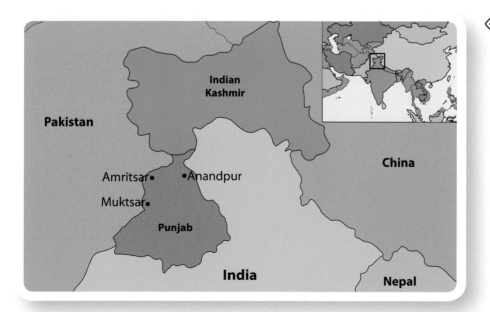

≪ Sikhs seek to understand more about Waheguru and the teachings of the Gurus.

Being a Sikh

Sikhs believe in living a good life. This means working hard and helping others. Sikh clothes and hair are outward signs of their beliefs. Adult Sikhs are expected to wear follow rules known as the Five Ks and wear a head covering. Male Sikhs wear a **turban**, which keeps their uncut hair tidy and shows respect for the Gurus.

The Khalsa and the Five Ks

Adult Sikh men and women go through an **initiation** ceremony to become members of the community called the **Khalsa,** which was founded by Guru Gobind Singh in 1699. Members of the Khalsa must have no other religion. The Guru taught that Sikh women and men should follow five rules to show they were members of the Khalsa:

- not cutting their hair
- carrying a comb
- carrying a curved sword
- wearing kaccha, or cotton trousers
- wearing a steel or iron bangle.

These rules are called the Five Ks because they all begin with "K" in the Punjabi language.

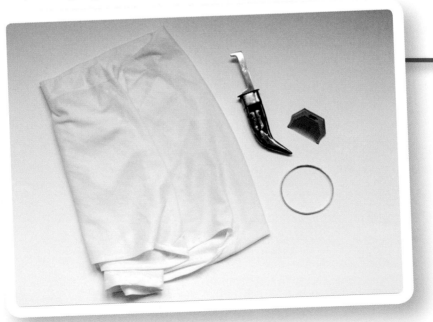

⌃ Sikhs normally wear ceremonial dress for special days and festivals. The kirpan sword or knife they carry is a sign of resistance against evil. In the past, Sikhs often had to defend themselves from enemies.

Sikh names

The 10 Gurus wanted Sikhs to be different from the **class** system they saw in Indian society at the time. Even surnames were a sign of social class.

Guru Gobind Singh decided that all male Sikhs should take the surname Singh (Lion) and all women should take the surname Kaur (usually translated as Princess). Some Sikh first names can be the same for men and women, but the surname Singh or Kaur prevents confusion.

Different kinds of festivals

Sikhs do not have a set holy day every week, unlike other religions. In Britain, they often worship on a Sunday because many people are not at work then.

Although Sikh festival days are not always as central to their worship as in other religions, celebrating Sikh history and beliefs is important. There are two kinds of festival. **Gurpurbs** mark the anniversaries of Gurus' birthdays and deaths. **Melas** are festivals that combine ceremony and celebration.

Celebrations with food

Sharing food is a central part of Sikh worship and celebrations. The **langar** is a meal served to anyone visiting a gurdwara at any time and is seen as part of worship.

The langar is also the name of the place in every gurdwara where food is prepared. The first Guru, Guru Nanak, started the tradition of Sikhs cooking and eating together. It shows that Sikhs do not believe in divisions between social classes or between men and women.

CALENDAR OF SIKH FESTIVALS

Today, most Sikhs use a calendar called the Nanakshahi calendar. Most festivals and special days fall on the same day every year according to the **Gregorian calendar** used in many countries.

Date in Nanakshahi Calendar	Festival
14 April	Vaisakhi, Guru Nanak's Birthday (see page 19)
16 June	Guru Arjan's martyrdom
1 September	Installation of Guru Granth Sahib
October/November	Diwali/Bandi Chhor Divas
24 November	Guru Tegh Bahadur's martyrdom
5 January	Guru Gobind Singh's Birthday
13 January	Maghi
March	Hola Mohalla

The first Sikh festivals

Festivals were not always a feature of the Sikh religion. Guru Amar Das, the third Guru, saw that Sikhs were enjoying the festivals of the Hindu religion. He ordered all Sikhs to gather in his presence at festival times. This created separate Sikh celebrations that happened at the same time as Hindu festivals.

⌃ The gurdwara is a meeting place as well as a place of worship.

VAISAKHI – NEW BEGINNINGS

Vaisakhi is the biggest and most important Sikh mela or festival. It is celebrated on 13 or 14 April. Vaisakhi marks the founding of the Khalsa in 1699, but it is also a celebration of Sikh New Year. Long before it became a Sikh festival, Sikhs would celebrate the harvest at this time. It was just before the start of the grain harvest in the Punjab.

Birth of the Khalsa

On Vaisakhi day 1699, Guru Gobind Singh called a meeting of Sikhs at his headquarters in the Indian city of Anandpur. He asked for five people who would volunteer to lay down their lives for the Sikh faith. Five men went into his tent. The crowd saw blood coming from his tent and believed the volunteers had been killed. However, they later came out unharmed.

The men were initiated into the Khalsa when they drank **amrit** and had it sprinkled on their eyes and hair. Amrit is still used in Sikh initiation ceremonies. Sikhs still see it as a great honour to take part in the amrit ceremonies today at Anandpur during Vaisakhi.

» This painting of Guru Gobind Singh is displayed in the city of Anandpur.

⌄ These young Sikhs in Birmingham, UK, are being sprinkled with amrit.

Now & Then

Holy places

For centuries, Sikhs have met at holy places such as the Golden Temple of Amritsar, also called Harmandir Sahib, to mark Vaisakhi. Some Sikhs celebrate by bathing in the waters of this holy city. Today, Sikhs around the world may listen to radio broadcasts from Amritsar.

Celebrating Vaisakhi

Vaisakhi is a day of ceremony and celebration at Sikh gurdwaras around the world. Gurdwaras and homes are specially decorated for the festival. Sikhs get up early and wear new clothes for the day. They will then visit their gurdwaras to sing religious songs and listen to readings from the Guru Granth Sahib.

Vaisakhi is a time for renewal and cleaning. The **Nishan Sahib** is the flag that flies over every gurdwara. At Vaisakhi, the chola, or covering, on the flagpole is taken down and washed. The pole itself is washed in yoghurt before the local community raise it again with a new Nishan Sahib.

⌃ Sikhs in California, USA, come together outside their gurdwara to clean the flagpole.

Marching through the street

The festival is marked by a **procession** through the street, called the Nagar Kirtan. The Guru Granth Sahib holy book is carried on the back of a truck or other large vehicle. The procession is led by five men in ceremonial dress. They are followed by the wider Sikh community, walking or riding on floats. The whole community will sing, accompanied by musicians.

Outside India, the Nagar Kirtan has become an annual celebration that shows others what it means to be a Sikh. In the UK, the procession in London attracts up to 75,000 people and there are similar celebrations in Birmingham and other cities with large Sikh communities.

Now & Then

Five beloved ones

Five men dressed in orange robes and carrying ceremonial swords lead the public procession of the Guru Granth Sahib at Vaisakhi. The Panj Pyare, meaning "five beloved ones", represent the first Sikhs who volunteered to lay down their lives for their religion in 1699.

Feasting and dancing

Eating together is always important for Sikhs and this is especially true at Vaisakhi.

After prayers and singing in the gurdwara, the community shares Karah Prasad, a special sweet dish (see page 40). Later, everyone will share a full meal in the langar area of the gurdwara.

Festival food

Vaisakhi began as a festival to celebrate the harvest. The delicious vegetarian food served during the festival reflects the plants and crops that are collected at this time. In the Sikh holy city of Amritsar, Vaisakhi is also a time for trade and selling farm animals.

⌃ Members of the community cook and serve the food in the gurdwara.

Food served at the gurdwara is always vegetarian, although anyone and everyone is welcome to share the meal, whether or not you are vegetarian. Sikhs are, however, allowed to eat meat.

In India, the feast will often be eaten outside, but this celebration is more likely to take place inside the gurdwara in the UK. In the UK, members of other religions are encouraged to join in public Vaisakhi celebrations of Sikh communities. Later, the party continues with music and dancing.

Now & Then

Ancient and modern music

The many poems and songs in the Guru Granth Sahib are all set to music. Gurdwara worship and Vaisakhi processions are often accompanied by traditional musicians called ragis. Ragis play drums, **harmonium** or lead the singing. Vaisakhi is a time for dancing and many young British Sikhs prefer to dance to modern **bhangra** music. This music has its roots in the energetic folk dances of the Punjab. However, it has been adapted by British Asians to feature Western instruments and rhythms.

▽ In India, Sikh men perform the traditional bhangra folk dance and women perform the **gidda** dance. These Sikhs are performing traditional dances in a dance contest.

Chickpea
curry

Since Vaisakhi is a harvest festival, people often eat vegetable curries for the holiday. Pindi chana (chickpea curry), popular in northern India, is a dish packed with protein – and spices!
See page 44 for more tips on this recipe!

TIME:

About 1 hour

SERVES:

4 people

TOOLS:

grater
spoons
knife and chopping board
strainer
medium saucepan
stirring spoon

Gluten Free

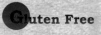

Dairy Free   Vegetarian

INGREDIENTS:

1 tablespoon vegetable oil
1 medium onion, finely chopped
1 teaspoon finely chopped garlic
2 teaspoons finely grated fresh ginger
2 tablespoons chopped, deseeded mild
        green chillies
¼ teaspoon salt
1½ teaspoon coriander
1½ teaspoon cumin
½ teaspoon turmeric
½ teaspoon garam masala
¼ teaspoon cayenne pepper
280 g chickpeas, drained and rinsed
2 large tomatoes, finely chopped
250 ml water
lemon, onion, tomato and fresh coriander
        leaves for garnish

Steps:

1 Heat the oil in the saucepan on medium heat. Add the onion and sauté for about 5 minutes until the onions are starting to brown.

2

Add the garlic, ginger, chillies, salt and spices. Sauté for about 3 minutes more.

3 Add the chickpeas, tomatoes and water. Turn the heat up to high. Bring the mixture to a boil, then reduce the heat and simmer for 20 to 30 minutes, uncovered, until there is no liquid left.

4 Garnish with lemon wedges, sliced onion, tomato wedges and chopped coriander.

GURPURBS

Gurpurbs are special days that celebrate the lives of the 10 Gurus. The Gurus led the Sikh community from its foundation until 1708, when Guru Gobind Singh died. After that, the Guru Granth Sahib became the Sikhs' teacher.

There are many gurpurbs throughout the year. Sikhs celebrate four in particular: the birthdays of Guru Nanak and Guru Gobind Singh, and the deaths of Guru Arjan and Guru Tegh Bahadur. The Guru Granth Sahib is celebrated with its own gurpurb.

Guru Nanak's birthday

As the Sikh religion is based on Guru Nanak's teachings, his birthday is the most widely celebrated of the Sikh gurpurbs.

⌃ Guru Nanak's birthday is celebrated at his birthplace near Lahore in Pakistan.

According to the Sikh Nanakshahi calendar, this special day is celebrated in April. However, Sikhs do not agree on the date. Many Sikhs celebrate their founder's birthday in November. Every year, Sikh **pilgrims** visit the gurdwara built in the city of Nankana Sahib in Pakistan, where Guru Nanak was born.

Guru Nanak's birthday is marked with early morning processions, singing and prayers in the gurdwara. These follow the end of the reading of the Guru Granth Sahib. The community then enjoys a shared meal at the gurdwara. People also meet for evening prayers at the local gurdwara.

Birthday parade

For the thousands of Sikhs living in Leicester, England, Guru Nanak's birthday is one of the biggest celebrations of the year. Crowds line the streets for a parade in honour of the first Guru. Sikhs taking part in the parade talk about the day as an opportunity for the whole community to get together.

⌃ Girls celebrate Guru Nanak's birthday at a street procession in Amritsar, India.

The spread of Sikhism

As more people in the Punjab became Sikhs, the **Mughal** kings of the region were unhappy about the growth of a religion different from their own religion, which was Islam. Emperor Jahangir arrested and killed Guru Arjan, who became the first Sikh **martyr**.

Sikhs remember the Guru on 16 June with ceremonies at gurdwaras. Cold drinks are often handed out to worshippers and passers-by, as a reminder of the thirst and suffering that the Guru suffered in his final days.

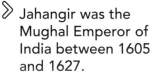
Jahangir was the Mughal Emperor of India between 1605 and 1627.

Gurpurbs are usually celebrated in the same way as the festival with Guru Arjan. They begin with a ceremonial reading of the holy book. Celebrations at the gurdwara include special sermons, singing and reciting poetry.

Remembering the holy book

On 1 September, Sikhs celebrate the installation of the Guru Granth Sahib. This gurpurb remembers the day in 1604 when the completed Sikh holy book was taken to Harmandir Sahib at Amritsar. This is also known as the Golden Temple, the holiest place of Sikhism. Reading from the Guru Granth Sahib is a part of every major Sikh event, including festivals.

Reading the Guru Granth Sahib

For 48 hours leading up to a gurpurb, Sikh communities organize a continuous reading of the Guru Granth Sahib. Each reader, who can be a man or woman, takes a two-hour turn to read part of the holy book. There is always another reader standing by to take over so the reading does not stop. Food is provided for the readers and other Sikhs who attend to listen. This **ritual** is called the akhand path. In large gurdwaras, there can be several readings going on at the same time.

A Guru martyr

Young Sikhs learn the stories of the Gurus they celebrate at gurpurbs. In 1675, Guru Tegh Bahadur became the second Guru to be martyred. He was executed in the city of Delhi on the orders of Emperor Aurangzeb.

A gurdwara now stands where Guru Tegh Bahadur died. According to Sikh history, he was executed because he tried to protect some Hindus from being forced to convert to Islam. The death of Guru Tegh Bahadur is remembered on 24 November.

The birthday of Guru Gobind Singh, the son of Guru Tegh Bahadur, is celebrated by Sikhs in January. This special day may include a service in which **hymns** written by the Guru are sung throughout the night.

≪ Guru Tegh Bahadur died in 1675. This gurdwara in Delhi, India, was built to remember him.

The 10 Gurus

Guru Nanak chose Guru Angad as his successor. Later Gurus were chosen from the sons or family members of the previous Guru. Sikhs believe that the Gurus were sources of the same teaching, so they are all equally important. The 10 Sikh Gurus served during the following dates:

Guru Nanak	Died in 1539	Guru Hargobind	Guru 1606–44
Guru Angad	Guru 1539–52	Guru Har Rai	Guru 1644–61
Guru Amar Das	Guru 1552–74	Guru Har Krishan	Guru 1661–64
Guru Ram Das	Guru 1574–81	Guru Tegh Bahadur	Guru 1664–75
Guru Arjan	Guru 1581–1606	Guru Gobind Singh	Guru 1675–1708

 A Sikh receives a drink of water in a gurdwara in Delhi, built to honour Guru Har Krisha.

Now & Then

Warrior Sikhs

When Guru Nanak founded Sikhism, most people in northern India were Hindus. Guru Nanak's parents were Hindus. The land was ruled by Mughal kings who followed Islam. These religious divisions led to conflict. In the 1600s, following the deaths of Guru Arjan and later Guru Tegh Bahadur, Guru Hargobind and Guru Gobind Singh urged Sikhs to take up arms and protect themselves. The kirpan or sword that Sikhs carry today dates from this time.

Diwali

The festival of Diwali is celebrated by Sikhs and Hindus in October or November. In areas where the two religions exist side-by-side, Sikh and Hindu families celebrate in similar ways. They may even enjoy the festival together. However, the meaning of the festival for Sikhs is different from the Hindu celebration. For Sikhs, it is about their religion's struggle for survival.

The day of release

Sikhs also call this festival Bandi Chhor Diwas, which means "the day of release of prisoners". This name dates from an event that took place in 1619.

The Mughal Emperor Jahangir had imprisoned Guru Hargobind, the sixth Guru. The Guru was offered freedom but refused it unless 52 Hindu prisoners could leave with him. The Emperor agreed, promising freedom to the prisoners who could hold on to Guru Hargobind's cloak as he left through a narrow doorway.

≪ Guru Hargobind recognized the need for the Sikh community to defend itself after the death of his father Guru Arjan.

The Guru attached long tassels to his cloak. This meant prisoners could grab on to them and win their freedom. Guru Hargobind arrived safely back at the Harmandir Sahib in Amritsar (see page 11). Sikhs celebrated by decorating the buildings of this holy city with lamps.

A festival of light

Diwali is a time of lights – for Sikhs and Hindus. In the past, the lights used at Diwali were traditional oil lamps, but now buildings are more likely to be decorated with electric lights. The night skies are lit up by fireworks and bonfires.

⌃ When Guru Hargobind arrived at Harmandir Sahib, Sikhs celebrated by decorating the Golden Temple and the pool around it with lamps. Today, there are still light displays there.

Diwali at Amritsar

Sikhs believe the city of Amritsar was founded at Diwali in 1577 by Guru Ram Das. Today, thousands of Sikhs gather there for the celebrations. Buildings are lit up by dazzling electric lights and food is freely available. Gurdwaras are filled for religious meetings lasting three days. Poets and musicians perform traditional Sikh songs.

Early in the morning, pilgrims in Amritsar bathe in the city's tanks, or lake. Later they take gifts to the Golden Temple, including money, flowers and sweets. In the evening, pilgrims gather for the amazing light shows. Lamps and candles float across the surface of the water.

⌃ Sikhs decorate their homes and gurdwaras for the Diwali celebrations.

Presents and cards

Sikhs can also celebrate the festival away from the holy city in northern India. Homes and gurdwaras are decorated in Sikh communities around the world. The festival is also a time for exchanging gifts. British Sikhs will often send cards to friends and family at Diwali. Young Sikhs have picked up this custom because of cards sent for birthdays and festivals by non-Sikh friends. Cards often have pictures of oil lamps or lights.

≫ Traditional presents at Diwali include specially made sweets.

Now & Then

A great meeting

In the 1700s, Vaisakhi and Diwali were times for the various groups of Sikh warriors to meet together. This was known as Sarbat Khalsa. For this, all members of the Khalsa assembled at Amritsar. The first Sarbat Khalsa took place at Diwali in 1723. Decisions made at these great meetings had to be followed by the whole Sikh community. More recently, a Sarbat Khalsa was organized in 1986. There have been other attempts to organize a great meeting to discuss issues affecting all Sikhs.

Fig and date
burfi

Sweets are one of the most important parts of a Diwali feast! Burfi comes in many forms. This mix of naturally sweet fruits, cut in a diamond shape, makes a tasty platter to serve to family and friends. **For tips on this recipe, see page 44.**

TIME:

About 45 minutes

SERVES:

Makes 24 burfi

TOOLS:

weighing scales
food processor
medium frying pan
stirring spoon
bowl
baking paper
knife and chopping board

 Vegetarian

Gluten Free

INGREDIENTS:

120 g dried figs
120 g pitted dates
2 tablespoons water
20 g unsalted butter
100 g mixed nuts, chopped (such as pistachios, almonds and cashews)
butter (to grease the baking paper)

STEPS:

1 In a food processor, **purée** the figs, dates and water into a paste.

2 Heat a frying pan on medium heat and melt the butter. Add the fig and date mixture. Cook for about 5 minutes.

3 Transfer the mixture to a bowl and let sit for about 5 to 10 minutes or until cool enough to handle. Then use your hands to mix in the chopped nuts.

4 Flatten the mixture onto a piece of buttered baking paper into a square shape, about 1–2 cm thick. Let it sit for about 15 minutes to harden.

5 With a knife, cut four to five strips horizontally across the burfi. Then cut diagonally to form diamond shapes. Carefully unpeel the burfi from the baking paper and place them on a plate to display … and share!

MAGHI

Maghi is another festival that commemorate a major event in Sikh history. Sikhs remember the death of 40 Sikh warriors who died trying to stop a Mughal army from capturing Guru Gobind Singh. The battle happened on the first day of the Indian month of Magh, which gives the festival its name. Nowadays, the festival is usually celebrated on 13 January.

Although Maghi marks a sad event, India's Sikhs still treat it as a festival. It takes place on the day after the Hindu festival of Lohri. The centre of Maghi is the town of Muktsar in the Punjab, where the battle took place.

Pilgrims travel to observe the festival in the streets and gurdwaras. They bathe in the sacred waters of the town. The festival ends with a procession to the main shrine of Guru Gobind Singh.

》 Maghi is also marked by a horse fair in Muktsar, when locally bred horses are bought and sold.

Sikhism and the Punjab

Almost all Sikhs can trace their family roots back to the Punjab region. The region is still at the centre of many Sikh festivals. The Gurus lived in the Punjab and the early battles of Sikhism were fought there, including the one at Maghi. Punjabi dress, food, music and dance are all part of Sikh festivals, whether they take place in Amritsar, Birmingham or New York.

In other places in the world, Maghi is not a big festival atteneded by everyone, like Vaisakhi or Diwali, though gurdwaras will still perform religious rituals and a reading of the Guru Granth Sahib, just as at many other Sikh festivals.

⌃ Sikhs have taken the traditional music and culture of the Punjab around the world, as shown by this festival celebration in Italy.

Hola Mohalla

Hola Mohalla is the third Sikh mela of the year, after Vaisakhi and Diwali. Like some other Sikh festivals, Hola Mohalla started as a Sikh alternative to an existing Hindu festival. This helped Sikhs to establish a strong separate identity in northern India.

Feast of strength

In 1680, Guru Gobind Singh, the tenth Guru, called for Sikhs to meet at his base of Anandpur during the Hindu festival of Holi. Holi is a joyous and colourful spring festival, but Hola Mohalla was much more serious when it was founded. The Sikhs who assembled at Anandpur in the Punjab were there for military training. They practised sieges, battles and other military exercises.

⌃ Today, the battles at Hola Mohalla are sporting contests.

Hola Mohalla today

Hola Mohalla is not celebrated as widely as Vaisakhi or Diwali. However, there is still a large fair every year at Anandpur. The fair lasts for three days, where Sikhs show their strength and skill with demonstrations such as bareback horse riding.

The fair is no longer just about physical exercise though. For example, Sikhs can listen to lectures and readings, and take part in music and dance competitions. On the last day, revellers at Anandpur form a procession, visiting many of the most important gurdwaras in the area. As always, food is cooked for everyone at the fair.

Now & Then

Sporting contests

Hola Mohalla is still a time for physical strength and competition between Sikhs, although without the military training that used to be a part of the festival. Nowadays, contests are more likely to be sports such as hockey, football or the Indian sport of kabaddi.

⚈ Kabaddi is a very popular sport in India and other South Asian countries.

FAMILY CELEBRATIONS

Family life is very important to Sikhs. Marriage and family are emphasized but, in many ways, Sikhs act as one big family. For example, they meet and share food at the gurdwara all year round.

It is no surprise that family celebrations are some of the most important festivals in the Sikh religion. They mark key points in the life of a Sikh, also called rites of passage. These include birth, becoming an adult, marriage and death.

Birth

The birth of a new baby is a time of great happiness for a Sikh family. The new parents show their joy by giving gifts of sweets to friends and neighbours. Family members also give presents to the new parents and their baby.

The newborn baby will be visited by a senior member of the local Sikh community, who mixes some water and sugar to make amrit (see page 10). A few drops of this special liquid are poured into the baby's mouth. This ritual sometimes takes place at the gurdwara.

Choosing a name

In many religions, parents will name a new baby after a member of the family, or pick a favourite name. In Sikh families, names are chosen at the gurdwara. The family takes the new baby to the gurdwara, where he or she is placed in front of the Guru Granth Sahib. Then the **Granthi**, who reads from the holy book, opens it at a random page. The baby's name will begin with the first letter of the first word on that page. This naming ceremony is also followed by adults who convert to Sikhism.

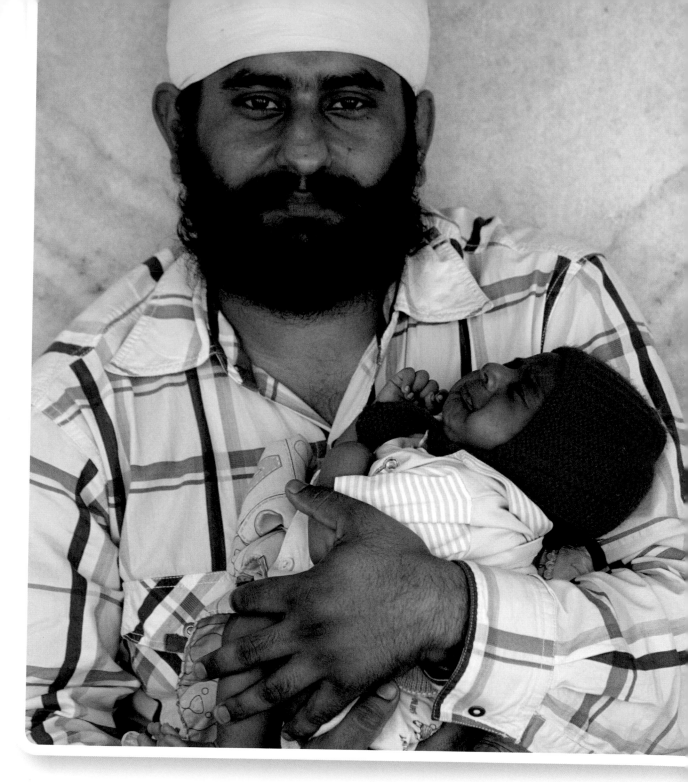

⌃ At a naming ceremony, a Sikh family will promise to bring up their child as a Sikh.

Tying the first turban

Adult male Sikhs usually wear turbans over their uncut hair to keep it clean and tidy. This cloth is usually 4–7 metres (13–23 feet) long and is wrapped round and round the head, covering up the man's uncut hair. Some female Sikhs also wear a turban, while others cover their uncut hair with a long scarf.

In their early teenage years, young Sikhs are taught to tie their first turban. This is a big step on the road to being an adult. It is marked by a ceremony called Dastar Bandi and a family celebration.

The ritual can happen at home or at the gurdwara. However, the turban is always tied in the presence of the Guru Granth Sahib. The child is taught to tie the turban by an older relative. Family and friends sing and play music.

Amrit ceremony

Older teenagers and adults become members of the Khalsa in the Sikh ceremony of taking amrit. This is a solemn ritual that takes place at the gurdwara.

The ceremony is conducted in a private room at the gurdwara, as only amritdhari (members of the Khalsa) and the candidates can be present. The candidates drink amrit that has been stirred with a double-edged sword. Amrit is also sprinkled over them as hymns and prayers are sung. Later, the whole **congregation** shares a meal of sweet-tasting Karah Prasad (see page 40).

The importance of the turban

The turban is an essential symbol of Sikhism. Its special significance for Sikhs in Britain has been accepted by the British government. For example, Sikhs do not have to wear motorcycle helmets, which would not fit over their turbans. Turbans are also allowed as an alternative to hard hats on building sites.

⌃ A young Sikh takes part in his Dastar Bandi ceremony in Washington DC, USA.

⋀ A Sikh wedding ceremony taking place in Hounslow,
near London.

Sikh weddings

All Sikhs are encouraged to marry and have a family, and the biggest family celebrations of all are Sikh weddings or Anand Karaj. Marriage is seen as the joining of two families. In some places, Sikh parents still wish to choose whom their sons and daughters will marry. However, some Sikh couples today meet and get married without their parents' direct involvement.

The wedding day

Before the wedding itself, the families meet for a meal called milni. They exchange gifts. When the groom arrives for the wedding, he may bring gifts for the bride's family. In India, the groom will often arrive on horseback. This sometimes happens at British Sikh weddings, too, although arriving by car is more usual.

The ceremony itself takes place in front of the Guru Granth Sahib in the gurdwara. Hymns and prayers are sung during the ceremony.

Then, the bride's father places flower garlands around the couple. He ties the end of a scarf worn by the groom to the bride's headscarf. This shows that the bride is leaving her father's family and joining her husband. The Sikh wedding hymn is sung and, during its four verses, the couple walk around the Guru Granth Sahib four times. After the ceremony, both families share a meal in the langar.

After the wedding

At the wedding reception, families and friends join in the music and dancing. After the reception, the families take part in the ritual of the bride leaving her family. She will return to the family home and the groom will follow to collect the bride. As she leaves, the bride throws a handful of rice over her shoulder. This is to wish luck and happiness to those who are seeing her leave.

∨ At some Sikh weddings, the bride's hands are decorated in elaborate patterns using henna dye.

Karah Prasad

Karah Prasad is a sacred dish, made with equal parts sugar, butter and flour. It is handed out to guests after special Sikh ceremony.

The cook recites prayers while making the pudding. Usually, the Karah Prasad is made with atta flour. However, you can use equal parts plain flour and wholemeal flour to achieve similar results.

See page 44 for more cooking tips.

TIME:

About 20 minutes

SERVES:

4 people

 Vegetarian

TOOLS:

kitchen scales
small saucepan
medium frying pan
stirring spoons

INGREDIENTS:

350 ml of water
120 g granulated white sugar
120 g unsalted butter
120 g flour (a mixture of 60 g plain flour
          and 60 g wholemeal flour)

STEPS:

Pour the water and sugar into the saucepan. Heat on medium until the sugar dissolves, for about 5 to 7 minutes.

1

2

In the frying pan, melt the butter on medium heat. Add the flour. Stir constantly, "toasting" the flour, for about 5 minutes.

Add the water and sugar mixture to the frying pan. Stir constantly, scraping the bottom and sides of the pan, as the flour mixture absorbs the water mixture.

3

The pudding will start to thicken (see picture). Soon, it will pull away from the sides of the pan. This will only take about 2 to 3 minutes.

4

5

Spoon into bowls and serve warm.

Death and funerals

The death of a loved one is always sad, but Sikhs try not to grieve too much. They believe that the person will be reborn or, if they have lived a good life, may live forever with Waheguru.

A dying person is visited by a Granthi, who reads to him or her from the Sikh holy book. Friends and family will also visit and read from the scriptures. They will sometimes bring gifts, such as specially prepared food.

⌃ Mourners attend a Sikh funeral in California, USA.

The dead person is dressed in the Five Ks (see page 6) for the funeral. In India, funerals are arranged as soon as possible after death, often on the same day.

Sikhs share the Hindu tradition of burning the body of the dead person on a funeral pyre. In Britain, Sikh funerals happen within a few days after a death, usually at a public **crematorium**. In India, this **cremation** usually takes place near a river and the ashes are scattered on the water.

Gurdwara and community

After the funeral, Sikhs return to the gurdwara, which is at the centre of so much Sikh life. Community and family are important to Sikhs, wherever they live in the world.

Beliefs about death

Sikhs believe that when someone dies, his or her spirit is reborn in another animal or human. Eventually a spirit may be released from this cycle of lives and go to join God. Whether this happens depends on the life the Sikh leads. The body itself is much less important and this is reflected in Sikh funeral ceremonies. Sikhs do not believe in putting up gravestones. They believe that the person's spirit is no longer connected to their previous body.

The gurdwara is at the centre of Sikh life, including a visit after a funeral.

COOKERY TIPS

Chickpea curry

- Dried spices can lose their smell and flavour if kept too long. The best place to store them is in an air-tight container in a kitchen cupboard. Spices stay freshest in dry, cool places out of sunlight.

- You can buy diced chillies in jars. If you use fresh ones, be careful when you chop them up. Chillies can irritate your skin and eyes. Cut open the chilli lengthwise (see picture above for what it should look like). Then remove the seeds and veins with a knife. The seeds contain a lot of the heat. Then rinse and dice the chilli into small pieces. When you are done, wash your hands thoroughly with warm soapy water.

- Sautéing cooks vegetables over high heat with a little bit of fat, such as vegetable oil. Doing this browns the vegetables and brings out their flavours before you add other ingredients.

Karah Prasad

- When you are cooking on the hob, always keep close watch and stir your ingredients often so they don't burn. Turn down the heat, if necessary. Always double check that you turn off the rings completely when you are finished.

TIMELINE

1469	Guru Nanak is born
1581	Guru Arjan becomes Guru. He puts together the first version of the Guru Granth Sahib, the Sikh holy book.
1604	Installation of Guru Granth Sahib at Amritsar
1606	Guru Arjan is killed for defending Sikhism
1619	First Sikh Diwali festival takes place after Guru Hargobind is released from prison
1675	Martyrdom of Guru Tegh Bahadur. Guru Gobind Singh becomes tenth Guru.
1680	First Hola Mohalla festival takes place at Anandpur
1699	Guru Gobind Singh founds the Khalsa
1708	Guru Gobind Singh, the last human Guru, dies
1911	The first gurdwara opens in the UK
1919	Many Sikhs are killed by British soldiers while celebrating Vaisakhi at Amritsar
1947	India gains independence from the UK. Punjab is divided between India and Pakistan, forcing Sikhs in Pakistan to flee to India.
1970s	Sikhs and others are forced to leave East Africa; many of them settle in the UK

GLOSSARY

amrit something you can drink, which is a mixture of sugar and water used in Sikh ceremonies

bhangra Punjabi dance traditionally performed by men. The word is now also used as the name of a type of pop music with a strong Indian influence.

class group of people within society who share similar backgrounds, such as level of wealth or education

congregation group of people in a place of worship, such as a gurdwara or church

cremation burning of the remains of a dead person

crematorium building where funeral services are held and bodies are cremated

gidda Punjabi dance traditionally performed by women

Granthi leading member of the Sikh community who reads scriptures during services

Gregorian calendar most widely used international calendar, also called the Western or Christian calendar

gurdwara Sikh place of worship

gurpurb festival marking the anniversary of a Guru's birth or death

guru important religious leader and teacher. In Sikhism, the 10 Gurus taught and led the Sikh community.

Guru Granth Sahib Sikh holy book

henna type of dye made from the leaves of a tropical plant. It is used to colour hair and to decorate the body.

harmonium instrument a little like a keyboard. Some of its sound is made by a pair of bellows (device with an air bag that inflates and deflates).

hymn religious song

initiation act of admitting someone into a society or group using a ritual or ceremony

Khalsa community of Sikh men and women who have been initiated during an amrit ceremony

langar meal served at the gurdwara, or the room where it is served

martyr someone who dies or is killed because of his or her beliefs

mela fair or a general festival

Mughal Muslim kings who ruled what is now India and Pakistan in the 16th to the 18th centuries

Nishan Sahib Sikh flag

pilgrim someone who travels to visit a particular place for religious reasons

procession parade of people or vehicles, often as part of a ceremony

Punjab region of northern India where the Sikh religion started and where most Sikhs live

purée to turn something into a smooth liquid or paste, usually in a food processor or blender

ritual religious ceremony or custom

spiritual describes deep feelings or beliefs, such as religious beliefs

turban long piece of cloth tied around the head to cover the hair

FIND OUT MORE

Books
Sikhism (Our Places of Worship), Honor Head (Wayland, 2009)
Sikhism (Special Times), Gerald Haigh (A & C Black, 2009)
Sikh Stories (Storyteller), Anita Ganeri (Tulip Books, 2013)
What Do You Believe? (Dorling Kindersley, 2011)

Websites
www.bbc.co.uk/schools/religion/sikhism
The BBC schools website has a section covering Sikhism.

sikhswolverhampton.org.uk/?q=node/24
The website of Wolverhampton's Sikh community includes a look inside a gurdwara.

Places to visit
There are Sikh communities in many cities in the UK and in other countries. Sikh gurdwaras are happy to welcome people of any religion. You could contact your local gurdwara to find out more about Sikhism. Here are some gurdwaras in the UK:

- Gurdwara Sri Guru Har Krishnan Sahib Ji, Manchester
- Glasgow Gurdwara
- Central Gurdwara (Khalsa Jattha), London

If you would like to visit a gurdwara, it is a good idea to contact them in advance. All gurdwaras would require you to take shoes off, wash your feet and cover your head before entering the main hall. You should always be quiet and respectful in any place of worship.

INDEX